Juices and smoothies
for kids

W9-CST-858

hamlyn

Juices and smoothies for kids

Healthy recipes that children will love

First published in Great Britain in 2007 by
Hamlyn, a division of Octopus Publishing Group Ltd,
2–4 Heron Quays, London E14 4JP

Copyright © Octopus Publishing Group Ltd 2007

All rights reserved. No part of this work may
be reproduced or utilized in any form or by
any means, electronic or mechanical, including
photocopying, recording or by any information
storage and retrieval system, without the prior
written permission of the publisher.

ISBN-13: 978-0-600-61621-4
ISBN-10: 0-600-61621-5

A CIP catalogue record for this book is available
from the British Library

Printed and bound in China

10 9 8 7 6 5 4 3 2 1

Both metric and imperial measurements
have been givem in all recipes. Use one set
of measurements only, and not a mixture
of both.

Standard level spoon measurements are
used in all recipes.
1 tablespoon = one 15 ml spoon
1 teaspoon = one 5 ml spoon

This book should not be considered as a
replacement for professional medical
treatment; a physician should be consulted
on all matters relating to health. While the
advice and information in this book is
believed to be accurate, neither the author
nor the publisher can accept any legal
responsibility for any illness sustained
while following the advice in this book.

Contents

Introduction

Do your kids refuse cabbage and turn their noses up at broccoli? Would they rather have a biscuit than an apple?

Yes? Well, it's all part of the ongoing battle between children and their parents when it comes to getting them to reach their five-a-day fruit and vegetable quota. They would far rather be tucking into an unhealthy packet of crisps or a bar of chocolate – after all, they're kids, what else would you expect?

It's no real wonder you have a fight on your hands. Food manufacturers the world over are out to manipulate your little ones into wanting drinks and snacks that have little or no nutritive value, and in all honesty, are creating all sorts of future health problems for a whole generation of growing, developing children.

Let's face it, to the taste-buds of a child, heavily advertised 'banana-flavoured' junk tends to beat a real banana hands down. It's full of addictive sugars, lots of hydrogenated fats and loads of salt, with a few additives thrown in for good measure. Added to which, all their friends in the playground are eating it, and they might even get one of the six collectable plastic cartoon characters free!

But that collectable cartoon character will be long gone by the time they join the growing number of teenagers being diagnosed with diabetes, or as young adults they find out they have developed cardiac problems or cancer. It certainly won't be able to help them cope with their schoolwork or get a good night's sleep; and when obesity damages their self-confidence and stops them from participating in physical activities that could help them feel healthier and better about themselves, they aren't going to derive any comfort from a long-forgotten childhood hero.

This may sound a little harsh, but unfortunately it is a serious problem that is getting worse. But luckily for many children, the adults who care for them are waking up to the reality that what they feed their kids today will have an impact – good or bad – on their tomorrows. With a lot of dedication, a bit of imagination and a touch of guile, you can improve the situation tremendously. The most important thing is to begin now, as the earlier you can get a children to enjoy fuelling their bodies with healthy natural food, the less chance they'll have of developing eating habits that will severely compromise their future wellbeing.

Your first strategy in this battle for good health should be to get them active and get them thirsty because the delicious juices and smoothies in this book will hit the spot, and instead of the usual refusals, you may even hear them asking for more.

Why juice?

Juicing has to be one of the most effective and easy ways to ensure your children hit their five-a-day target of fruits and vegetables and reap the benefits of the vitamins, minerals, phytonutrients and enzymes that these natural powerhouses contain.

Five reasons to have five-a-day

1 Raw energy It's better to consume most fruits and vegetables raw because cooking destroys many of the vital enzymes that are so fundamental to optimum health. A growing child is reliant on a diet rich in these enzymes in order to maintain a healthy metabolism, to digest and convert food into body tissue, and to produce sufficient energy for the day ahead.

2 Immune booster Eating plenty of colourful fruits and vegetables is an insurance policy that guards against bugs and infections and helps prevent future degenerative diseases, as the phytonutrients they contain detoxify the body, combat free radicals and are essential for an effective immune system.

3 Instant hit The nutrients in fruits and vegetables are usually released when the digestive process separates them from the indigestible fibre. However, they are assimilated far more quickly and in larger quantities when you juice them.

4 Rehydration Fruits and vegetables contain large amounts of water – a vital requirement of the human body as we are made up of around 60 per cent H_2O ourselves, and those levels constantly need replenishing, particularly in active children. Fizzy drinks tend to dehydrate the body, so juices are a great choice.

5 All natural Why would you even contemplate giving a child a drink that is full of dangerous additives, caffeine and high levels of sugar or artificial sweeteners, when the real thing tastes so much better and actually does them a power of good? A little effort now will be well worth it in the long run.

Become a rainbow warrior

In order to ensure you are getting the best nutritional combination of vitamins, minerals, antioxidants and phytochemicals, make sure that you eat red, green, yellow, orange and purple fruits and vegetables. Get your children involved in picking out a colourful range of produce when you go shopping. Creating interest at this stage will help make them enthusiastic when it comes to actually making and drinking the juices and smoothies. You could even create a different colour juice rota for each day of the week and get them to mark off when they have had their daily dose of green, yellow, red, purple, etc. Make it fun as well as healthy.

Why buy organic?

Long gone are the years where everything was grown in naturally fertilized soils and fruits and vegetables were eaten in season. The nutritional picture today is a very different one:

- Fields are sprayed with herbicides, pesticides and fungicides.
- Intensive farming methods are stripping the soil of vital minerals.
- Demand for out-of-season fruits and vegetables means they are being picked before they ripen, then transported and stored in refrigerated containers. By the time they reach supermarket shelves the nutritional value has already been stripped.
- Organic produce is grown in sustainable farming conditions – no pesticides, artificial ingredients, preservatives or irradiation.

If dealing with fruits and vegetables of unknown origin always:

- Remove skins of citrus fruits that may have been waxed.
- Peel non-organic hard fruits and vegetables before juicing, or wash in warm water with a little washing-up liquid, rinse very thoroughly and dry.
- Wash all berries and leaves before using.

Utilize your freezer when organic produce such as berries, melons, pineapples, bananas, grapes and exotic fruit such as mangoes and papaya are available. Simply wash berries, peel and chop fruit where necessary, then freeze on large trays overnight, and transfer to freezer containers or bags the next day. This ensures that the fruits are kept separate and easy to remove – rather than one large frozen lump.

How to juice

The first step towards incorporating healthy juices and smoothies into your child's diet is to equip yourself with the proper appliances for the job.

Spend as much as you can afford on good quality machines from a reputable manufacturer. Cheaper ones may seem a bargain but all too often they break down after regular use. Experience tells that the cheaper the juicer, invariably the lower quality the resulting juice. A good quality juicer will extract more of the nutrients held in the peel, pith and pips of certain fruits and vegetables so you can benefit from the full range of goodness they have to offer.

Blender

Look for a jug blender that has a variety of speeds as you will need to be able to crush ice and blend frozen fruit.

Juicers

There are two main types of juicer. Whichever type you choose, a key point to note is that the drier the pulp, the more effective the juicer.

Centrifugal: This is the most widely used and affordable juicer. Fruits and vegetables are fed into a rapidly spinning grater and the juice and pulp are separated.

Masticating: The larger, more expensive juicers are usually masticating or pulverising. The fruits and vegetables are pushed through a wire mesh – this action is very powerful and produces a high level of juice with very dry pulp. Compared to the centrifugal juicer, the juice contains more nutrients as not only is there more of it, but it hasn't been extracted via a spinning metal blade, which produces heat, which in turn kills those vital enzymes.

Pulp Action

Rather than throw away the fruit and vegetable pulp, it can be added to smoothies, muffins, soups, casseroles, meat dishes, etc. for added nutrition and fibre. If freezing, remember to add a little lemon juice.

Juicing hints

- Use fresh and firm fruits and vegetables for maximum nutrient content.
- Wash or scrub all fruits and vegetables thoroughly.
- Remove all stems and large stones.
- Pass fruits and vegetables through the juicer slowly and steadily using the pusher provided – never use knives or other metal kitchen implements, and if your children are helping, make sure they are supervised.
- Do not cut fruits and vegetables too small – ideally cut them to a size that fits comfortably into the chute.
- When juicing leafy vegetables, roll them into a ball and push through followed by harder fruit or vegetables, which will also help push through softer fruits.
- Don't try to juice bananas, avocados or very over-ripe fruit – this will clog up the juicer. Use these in smoothies instead.
- The most aggravating aspect of juicing is cleaning the machine after use – this has to be done immediately you have finished juicing, and it has to be done thoroughly as any residue will harbour bacterial growth. For this reason, look out for a machine that dismantles easily.
- Most machines come with a special brush to clean the mesh or grater. Wire cleaning pads are excellent for the job.

Homemade ice lollies can be a healthy treat if made with natural fruit juice. Many of the recipes in this book are suitable for freezing.

Juice Yield

Juice yields will vary slightly according to the machine used and ripeness and size of certain fruits but in general the icons in this book represent the following volumes.

1 standard glass (approx 200 ml/7 fl oz)

1 small glass (approx 150 ml/5 fl oz)

1 ice lolly (approx 75 ml/3 fl oz)

The volume of ice lolly moulds depends on the brand. Allow for a slight variation in the number of ice lollies each recipe makes.

Top fruits and vegetables for juices and smoothies

Fruits

Apples are a great juicing ingredient. They cleanse the digestive system and boost the immune system. They provide an excellent base for many juices, and even a small addition of apple will soften the taste of a stronger vegetable blend.

Apricots are a tasty addition to smoothies - either dried, fresh or tinned in their own juices. They are full of minerals and vitamins, especially vitamin A, immune boosting beta-carotene and calcium. Apricots are also a very good source of iron.

Bananas are one of the classic smoothie staple ingredients, renowned for their energy-giving properties when you are busy and on the run and the ability to induce calm due to their high tryptophan content. They make a delicious ice-cream substitute if pulped and frozen.

Blackcurrants are antiviral and antibacterial as they are full of vitamin C. They mix brilliantly with apple and have a flavour that children love.

Blueberries are a natural cure for diarrhoea and will have a settling effect on upset tummies. As with all berries, buy in bulk when they are in season and freeze.

Cherries contain powerful antioxidants. They don't contain loads of juice so are better used in smoothies. They are a good source of folic acid, vitamin C and calcium.

Cranberries are both antiviral and antibiotic but they are very sour, so must be combined with sweeter fruit in juices and smoothies.

Grapes, whether red or green, are intensely sweet and easy to juice and they will take the edge off slightly bitter vegetables. Their high glucose content makes them an effective boost for flagging children, and high levels of potassium make them ideal after exercise.

Kiwifruits are full of fibre and packed with vitamin C that accelerates general healing and boosts the immune system.

Mangoes boost the body's defences as their high levels of vitamins A and C and beta-carotene prevent damage to cells by free radicals, and they add fruity sweetness to citrus-based smoothies.

Melons are a highly nutritious ingredient. They are natural diuretics, powerful cleansers and detoxifiers. Because of their high water content they are also great for rehydration.

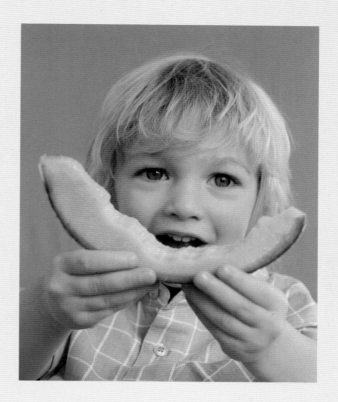

Oranges contain carotenoids, bioflavonoids and huge levels of vitamin C. Citrus fruits are antiviral, antibacterial and extremely versatile and flavoursome.

Papaya is the tops when it comes to aiding digestion as it contains the enzyme papain. This helps to break down protein. It also replenishes lost levels of vitamin C.

Peaches have a gentle laxative effect on the system and are good for calming irritated stomachs. Puréed peach with a little lemon and honey makes a great natural cough mixture.

Pear juice is fabulous if you are weaning a child as it very rarely causes an allergic reaction. It is great for slow energy release and, when combined with prunes or peaches, it is an effective laxative.

Pineapples are anti-inflammatory, antiviral and antibacterial and contain the digestive enzyme bromelain which is essential in the digestion of protein. Avoid drinking pineapple juice by itself as it can be damaging to tooth enamel.

Raspberries contain natural aspirin and add great colour to juices and smoothies. They can be slightly sharp so combine with more mellow fruits to create child-friendly drinks that may help take the pain away.

Strawberries will help keep your child from becoming anaemic as they are high in vitamin C and folate which is necessary for red blood cell manufacture. Whether in juices or smoothies strawberries are a popular choice with children.

Vegetables

Avocados are a complete food, packed with essential nutrients. Their high vitamin E content is excellent for maintaining a healthy skin, wound healing, and, of course, bolstering the immune system.

Bean and seed sprouts contain high levels of nutrients that are easy for the body to absorb. They are super foods with a high protein, enzyme, vitamin and mineral content. They protect against cancer and support every system in the body.

Beetroots are high in folate which is necessary for red blood cell manufacture. They have a regulating effect on the digestive system, stimulate and strengthen the bowel, moving toxins out of the system. Kidney and liver function can be improved and the blood cleaned and fortified by regular consumption of beetroot, which is very sweet and mixes well with berries when juiced.

Broccoli is a member of the cruciferous family of vegetables. These are loaded with antioxidants and broccoli is pulsating with vitamin C. It is fantastic when mixed with very sweet fruits, such as apple and pineapple.

Carrots are nutritional powerhouses with a very high beta-carotene content. They battle infections and boost immunity. Carrots are also effective against macular degeneration and blend well with virtually all other ingredients.

Celery is a natural detoxifier and is great for cleansing the digestive system. It has a high potassium content so is brilliant for rehydration.

Cucumber is a good base for many refreshing juices and smoothies. It is naturally diuretic and will stimulate elimination of toxins via the urinary tract. It also contains compounds essential for healthy hair and skin nutrition.

Lettuce contains high levels of vitamin C, beta-carotene, flavonols and folic acid. Vary the lettuce you choose to juice as they all have slightly different phytonutrients. Essentially all have antioxidant properties, cleanse the

digestive tract and enhance the activity of bacteria in the gut. A good choice to include in children's juices as it is relatively mild tasting.

Spinach is one of the leafy vegetables that should be an integral part of the daily diet as they are all rich in antioxidants, beta-carotene and calcium. Mix spinach with sweeter fruit-based juices a couple of times every week for a great bone-building boost.

Tomatoes have got to be the best, most versatile ingredient known to man, and so fantastic for our health. They lower the risk of cancer and heart disease as the presence of lycopene fights off free radicals. Even though some children don't like them, they do mix well with most other fruits, so can be disguised.

What not to juice

Fruits and vegetables not suitable for juicing are:

Aubergines – a member of the deadly nightshade family which should never be eaten raw as they contain a toxin called solanine which may cause diarrhoea, heart failure, headache and vomiting in some sensitive people.

Coconut – it will produce virtually no juice and almost definitely damage the juicer in the process.

Leeks – simply don't juice well, but there is nothing wrong with eating young, tender ones raw.

Rhubarb – it contains high levels of kidney-damaging oxalic acid that is only removed by cooking.

Fruity favourites

This deliciously refreshing juice has a high vitamin C content to ward off colds, so administer at the first sign of sniffles. Strawberries are natural painkillers and oranges are full of potassium which is vital for rehydration, making this juice a good choice after tiring play. Freeze the liquid to make a great ice lolly for sore throats.

Strawberry sunrise

200 g (7 oz) **strawberries**

2 **oranges**

Hull the strawberries. Peel the oranges and divide the flesh into segments, then juice with the strawberries. Serve straight over ice, or whiz in a blender with a couple of ice cubes to make a cooling smoothie. Decorate with sliced strawberries, if liked.

MAKES

Good source of vitamin C, potassium and calcium

Packed with iron, calcium and potassium, this all-round booster is great for bones and teeth. It is also really energizing and when combined with a protein snack such as nuts and seeds it will keep busy kids on the go.

Fireball

1 **ripe mango**
½ **Galia melon**
200 ml (7 fl oz) **orange juice**

Peel the mango, remove the stone and roughly chop the flesh. Peel the melon, deseed and roughly chop the flesh. Place the mango and melon flesh in a blender. Add the orange juice and a couple of ice cubes, then purée until smooth. Serve immediately.

MAKES

Good source of vitamins A and C, selenium and zinc

A natural vitamin tonic that helps to support the immune system and keep bugs at bay. This makes a fantastic breakfast juice bolstered by the addition of kiwifruits which contain even more vitamin C than oranges, so by combining the two fruits you are giving your children an even more potent dose.

Double C

2 **large oranges**
3 **kiwifruits**, peeled

Peel the oranges, leaving on as much pith as possible, and juice them along with the kiwifruits. Serve over ice.

MAKES

Good source of vitamins A and C, potassium and folic acid

Apples are naturally cleansing so they are great for a young digestive system that has over-indulged in too much 'party food'. If you whiz the juice in a blender with a couple of prunes it can also alleviate constipation.

Tummy tickler

300 g (10 oz) **apple,** such as Braeburn or Gala

200 g (7 oz) **blackcurrants**

Juice the fruit and serve over ice for a great blackcurrant cordial substitute. Decorate with extra blackcurrants.

MAKES

Good source of vitamin C, calcium, copper, zinc and iron

This is the perfect juice for the young extreme sportsperson as it is high in energy-giving carbohydrates and, more importantly, the B vitamins needed to release that energy. Pineapple also helps digestion, due to the enzyme bromelain that breaks down protein.

Sky high

2 **pears**
½ **lemon**
200 g (7 oz) **fresh pineapple,** or
canned in its own juices

If using fresh pineapple, peel and cube the flesh. Juice all the fruit and serve over ice.

MAKES

Good source of vitamins B_1, B_6 and C, calcium, zinc and copper

Weight for weight, kiwifruits contain more vitamin C than oranges. Ensuring that there is enough vitamin C in your child's diet is vital for general healing since it plays a major role in most bodily functions.

Crazy kiwi

2 **ripe pears**
3 **kiwifruits**

Wash the pears and peel the kiwifruits. Slice the fruit into even-sized pieces, then juice. Pour the juice into a glass, add a couple of ice cubes if desired and decorate with slices of kiwifruit.

MAKES

Good source of vitamins C and B$_6$, copper, magnesium, phosphorus and calcium

An excellent summertime refresher, especially when the sun-ripened berries are at their most plentiful. Buy extra and freeze so you can inject a little summer sunshine all year round. The calcium and iron content helps to prevent fatigue. Makes a good ice lolly for sore throats.

Berry bouncer

100 g (3½ oz) **strawberries**
75 g (3 oz) **redcurrants**
½ **orange**
125 ml (4 fl oz) **water**
½ teaspoon **clear honey** (optional)

Hull the strawberries and redcurrants, and peel the orange. Juice the fruit and add the water. Stir in the honey, if using. Pour into lolly moulds and freeze. If serving as a drink add ice cubes if desired and decorate with redcurrants, if liked.

MAKES

Good source of vitamins C, B_1 and B_2, niacin, B_6, folic acid, copper, potassium, calcium, magnesium and phosphorus

This juice is high in natural carbohydrates which are essential for growing children. It is especially good before exercise as it is a great energy provider. As the mango is full of sweetness you can use fairly tart varieties of apple, such as Worcester.

3 **apples,** preferably red
2 **passionfruits**
1 **mango**

Wash the apples and chop them into even-sized pieces. Slice the passionfruits in half, scoop out the flesh and discard the seeds. Peel the mango and remove the stone. Juice all the ingredients. Pour the juice into glasses and add some ice cubes.

MAKES ⎕⎕

Good source of vitamins A and C, potassium, magnesium, phosphorus and iron

High carb, mineral rich and a beautifully sweet energizing fuel for kids on the go, this is perfect for sports fans and busy little bees. Tart apples such as Granny Smiths provide a good counterbalance to the melon and pineapple, and the high water content of the melons makes this juice very refreshing.

Go green

½ **Galia melon**
¼ **pineapple**
3 **green apples**

Remove the skin and seeds from the melon. Remove the skin and hard core from the pineapple. Chop all the fruit into even-sized pieces and juice. Pour into a glass and add a couple of ice cubes.

MAKES

Good source of vitamins C, B_1, B_2 and B_6, copper, potassium, magnesium, phosphorus and calcium

This is a good drink to have with a lunch as the bromelain helps to break down protein and the B vitamins are necessary to release energy from carbohydrates. It will keep kids going until teatime.

Yellow submarine

¼ **pineapple**

2 **pears**

Peel the pineapple and remove the core. Chop all the fruit into even-sized pieces and juice it. Pour into a glass and add a couple of ice cubes.

MAKES

Good source of vitamins C, B_1 and B_6, calcium, iron and copper

If you choose plums that are ripe but not overripe, you will find it easier to remove the stones before juicing. Plums contain potassium and iron and have laxative properties, and this juice will guarantee your child gets more than the recommended apple a day.

Plum scrumpy

5 **ripe plums**
3 **red apples**

Slice the plums into quarters and remove the stones. Cut the apples into even-sized pieces. Juice the fruit and serve in a glass over a couple of ice cubes.

MAKES

Good source of vitamins A, C and B_6, niacin, copper and potassium

The wonder of this golden nectar is how full of beta-carotene, vitamin C and iron it is. The vitamin C helps the absorption of the iron which makes it an ideal choice for any child feeling a little below par.

Golden wonder

3 **apricots**
1 large **nectarine** or **peach**
2 **passionfruits**
150 ml (¼ pint) **apple juice,** freshly pressed

Cut the apricots in half and discard the stones. Cut the nectarine or peach in half and discard the stone. (If your children don't like 'bits', peel the fruit before you start.) Cut the passionfruits in half, scoop out the pulp and strain through a sieve to remove the seeds. Put everything in a blender with a couple of ice cubes and whiz until smooth.

MAKES

Good source of vitamins A and C, iron and potassium

This juice will help get your child through the day as it contains large amounts of carbohydrate for energy release, plus a hefty amount of vitamin C which helps to increase oxygen uptake and energy production. Try combining it with a protein snack such as cheese to regulate blood sugar and maintain consistent performance.

Battery charge

2 **kiwifruits**
300 g (10 oz) **seedless green grapes**

Peel the kiwifruits and juice them with the grapes. Pour the juice into a glass and add a couple of ice cubes. Decorate with kiwifruit slices, if liked.

MAKES

Good source of vitamins C, B_1 and B_6, copper, potassium, magnesium, phosphorus and calcium

This is a good juice to include in the sports kit as it is isotonic – it replenishes potassium levels and quenches thirst. Grapes are a good source of glucose and fructose and make the perfect energy snack.

Kick start

150 g (5 oz) **Galia melon**
75 g (3 oz) **seedless green grapes**
150 ml (¼ pint) **water**

Peel the melon and deseed the flesh. Juice the melon and grapes. Add the water, pour into a glass and add ice cubes.

MAKES

Good source of vitamins A, C, B₁ and B₆, magnesium, phosphorus copper and potassium

A high water content and high glycaemic value makes this a perfect juice to drink before exercise. As well as copious amounts of vitamin C, it provides potassium, which is vital for muscle and nerve function and might relieve tired legs.

Red devil

300 g (10 oz) **watermelon** (flesh from ¼ of an average fruit)

125 g (4 oz) **raspberries**

Remove the skin and deseed the watermelon. Chop the flesh into pieces. Juice all the fruit, pour it into a glass and some crushed ice cubes if desired.

MAKES

Good source of vitamins C and B$_6$, folic acid, calcium, copper and potassium

Cranberries may not seem an obvious choice for children as they are very sour, but they are so rich in vitamin C that it is worth including them in juices and smoothies. This juice partners the sweetness of the mango and orange with a spoonful of honey to counteract the sharpness of the berries and rev up the vitamin C content even further. When fresh cranberries are not in season, use frozen cranberries instead, but defrost them first.

Sweet and sour

1 **mango**
1 **orange**
125 g (4 oz) **cranberries**
100 ml (3 ½ fl oz) **water**
1 teaspoon **clear honey**

Peel the mango and remove the stone. Peel the orange and divide the flesh into segments. Juice all the fruit, pour the juice into a glass and stir in the water and honey. Add a couple of ice cubes if desired and drink immediately.

MAKES

Good source of vitamins A, C, B₁ and B₆, copper, potassium, calcium and iron

A sweet juice full of carbohydrates and calcium, this is perfect for revving up flagging energy levels. Try serving it with a nutty snack bar or a handful of almonds and your child will soon be revived and leaping around.

Frisky frog

2 **kiwifruits**
375 g (12 oz) **honeydew melon**
125 g (4 oz) **seedless green grapes**

Put one peeled kiwifruit into a blender and process until smooth. Spoon into the base of the lolly moulds and freeze until set.

Remove the skin and deseed the melon. Peel the second kiwifruit. Chop the melon and kiwifruits into even-sized pieces. Juice all the fruit then pour it into the ready-frozen lolly moulds and freeze until solid.

MAKES

Good source of vitamins C, B$_6$ and B$_1$, copper, potassium, magnesium, phosphorus and calcium

This cooling juice supplies almost a complete daily quota of beta-carotene. This is converted by the body into vitamin A which is vital for healthy growth and development.

Princess peachy

3 **apricots**
1 **peach**
2 **apples**

Halve and stone the apricots and peach. Juice the apples, apricots and peach. Pour the juice into a blender with a few ice cubes and whiz for 10 seconds. Serve in a tall glass.

MAKES

Good source of vitamins A and C, magnesium, iron and zinc

Apple and blackberry are a classic combination, but blackberries can be tart so it is best to choose a sweet variety of apple, such as Braeburn, Pink Lady, Cox's Orange Pippin or Golden Delicious. Blackberries are a good source of vitamin E which is necessary for healing both inside and out, making this juice a liquid band aid for all those cuts and grazes.

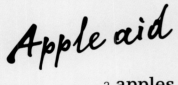

3 **apples**
150 g (5 oz) **blackberries**
300 ml (½ pint) **water**

Slice the apples into even-sized pieces. Juice the fruit, then stir in the water. Serve over ice cubes.

MAKES

Good source of vitamins C, B$_6$ and E, copper, magnesium, phosphorus, and calcium

Melons are full of carotenoids and blackberries a great source of anthocyanidins. Your children might not be able spell these powerful phytonutrients, but rest assured that this antioxidant punch will put the colour back in their cheeks.

Time out

100 g (3½ oz) **cantaloupe melon,** cubed

100 g (3½ oz) **blackberries,** fresh or frozen

2 **kiwifruits**

100 ml (3½ fl oz) **apple juice**

Juice the melon, blackberries and kiwifruits (no need to peel them), then put them in a blender with the apple juice and process with a couple of ice cubes. Pour into a glass and serve. Decorate with a few blackberries.

MAKES

Good source of vitamins A and C and magnesium

When the temperatures are soaring, prepare this great summer cocktail bursting with vitamin C. It is a perfect treat for a group of hot and sticky kids.

Strawberry and cherry sparklers

150 g (5 oz) **strawberries**
125 g (4 oz) **fresh cherries**
125 g (4 oz) **watermelon**
100 ml (3½ fl oz) **orange juice**
500 ml (17 fl oz) **sparkling water,** chilled

Hull the strawberries. Halve and pit the cherries. Deseed the watermelon and cut it into small chunks. Put all the fruit in a blender with the orange juice and blend until smooth. If you child will not like 'bits' in his or her drink, sieve the fruit purée over a bowl to remove the pips, skin and seeds. Pour the purée into the glasses. Top up with the sparkling water.

MAKES

Good source of vitamin C, calcium, magnesium, potassium and beta-carotene

If your child is under the weather and can't face food, maybe this simple juice will hit the spot and help them on the road to recovery. The addition of honey gives a much needed energy boost and the vitamin C content will help their struggling immune system.

Hug in a glass

2 **oranges**
1 **red apple**
1 **pear**
1 teaspoon **clear honey** (optional)

Peel the oranges and divide the flesh into segments. Chop the apple and pear into even-sized pieces. Juice all the fruit and pour it into a glass. Stir in the honey, if using, and add a couple of ice cubes if desired.

MAKES

Good source of vitamins C, B_1, B_2 and B_6, folic acid, calcium, copper, potassium, magnesium and phosphorus

With isotonic juices like this, you can confidently throw away commercial cordials and drinks high in additives and sugar. Refreshing, revitalizing and full of vitamin C, this will sustain – not drain – your child.

Raspberry crush

2 **large oranges**
175 g (6 oz) **raspberries**
250 ml (8 fl oz) **water**

Peel the oranges and divide the flesh into segments. Juice all the fruit, then add the water. Pour the juice into glasses and add a couple of ice cubes, if desired.

MAKES ⌴⌴⌴

Good source of vitamins C, B_6 and B_1, folate, zinc, copper, calcium, iron and potassium

Iron deficiency in children is a nutritional problem worldwide. This juice provides useful amounts of this important mineral, which helps transport oxygen around the body, and aids overall performance both in the classroom and on the sports field.

Iron kid

2 **peaches**
300 ml (½ pint) **water**
1 **red apple**
125 g (4 oz) **strawberries**

Remove the stones from the peaches, chop them into even-sized chunks and juice. Add one third of the water and divide evenly between the lolly moulds. Freeze until just set. Chop the apples into even-sized chunks and juice. Add one third of the water; pour on top of the frozen peach mixture then freeze until just set. Hull the strawberries then juice them. Add the remainder of the water, pour on top of the frozen apple mixture then freeze until set.

MAKES 🍭🍭🍭

Good source of vitamin C, copper, potassium, magnesium, phosphorus and iron

This juice packs a mighty anti-viral punch as it is full of vitamin C. Dispense at regular intervals along with the chicken soup and cuddles when your child is a little under the weather. One juice daily will help to keep those bugs and viruses away.

Doctor, doctor

2 **oranges**

1 **kiwifruit**, peeled

200 g (7 oz) **strawberries**

Peel the oranges and divide the flesh into segments. Roughly chop the kiwifruit, reserving a piece for decoration. Hull the strawberries. Juice the fruit. Serve in a tall glass with ice and a chunk of kiwifruit.

MAKES

Good source of vitamin C, potassium, magnesium and calcium

As well as being a vitamin-enriched tonic, this juice is an excellent natural laxative. For added potency, stir in a couple of tablespoons of prune juice and serve with a handful of pumpkins seeds to nibble on. Soon the whole system will be running smoothly.

2 **pears**
2 **apples**

Roughly chop the pears and apples, including the cores. Juice the apples and pears, then whiz in a blender with a couple of ice cubes. Pour into a tall glass and serve.

MAKES

Good source of vitamin C, potassium, magnesium and pectin

Run rabbit run

Vital veg

If your child likes a touch of spice, add a little fresh root ginger to this tasty combination, which benefits the immune system, supports good eyesight and provides selenium and zinc for a brain power boost.

Captain Zinger

250 g (8 oz) **cantaloupe melon**

1 **lime**

125 g (4 oz) **carrot**

1 cm (½ in) piece **fresh root ginger**

Peel, deseed and cube the melon. Peel the lime. Juice the carrot, melon, lime and ginger. Serve in a glass, over ice if desired.

MAKES

Good source of vitamins A and C, selenium and zinc

Sprouts are newly germinated seeds and pulses. These baby plants are bursting with all the nutrition needed to produce a fully grown plant – anti-oxidants, vitamins, minerals and trace elements – what better ingredients to give a growing child?

Green dream

3 **celery sticks**

2 **apples**, tart-flavoured, such as Granny Smith

25 g (1 oz) **alfalfa sprouts**

Cut the celery and apples into even-sized pieces. Rinse the alfalfa. Feed all the ingredients into a juicer in alternating batches. Pour into a glass, add a couple of ice cubes and drink immediately.

MAKES

Good source of vitamins A, C, B_6 and K, potassium, folic acid, iron and calcium

Juices give instant energy, so they are fabulous when little ones are getting a bit lethargic. Turn off the television, give them a juice, then send them out for a burst of fresh air. It will put a bloom back on their cheeks.

Power pack

125 g (4 oz) **strawberries**
250 g (8 oz) **carrot**
125 g (4 oz) **beetroot**
1 **orange**

Hull the strawberries. Juice the carrot, beetroot and orange and whiz in a blender with the strawberries and a few ice cubes. Decorate with a strawberry.

MAKES 🥛🥛

Good source of vitamins A and C, potassium, magnesium and selenium

This juice is sweet enough for a child to enjoy, especially with the addition of orange. Perhaps prepare it as a starter before a meal, or serve with lunch – a godsend for kids who won't eat vegetables.

Juice boost

4 **tomatoes**

2 **oranges,** peeled

2 **celery sticks,** plus
    leafy stalks

2 **carrots**

Juice all the ingredients, except for the leafy stalks. Pour the juice over ice cubes in glasses and serve with leafy celery stalk stirrers.

MAKES ⊔⊔

Good source of vitamin C, beta-carotene, potassium, lycopene, folate and sodium

This is a great juice for your child to help you make, as they can cast a spell as they clean and chop – carrots to help you to see, an orange to scare away colds and an apple a day to keep the doctor away.

Magic juice

2 **carrots,** about 200 g (7 oz) in total

1 **orange**

1 **apple**, tart-flavoured, such as Granny Smith

Scrub the carrots. Peel the orange and divide into segments. Cut the carrots and apple into even-sized pieces. Juice all the fruit, pour it into a glass, then add a couple of ice cubes, if liked.

MAKES

Good source of vitamins C, B$_1$ and B$_6$, beta-carotene, folic acid, potassium, calcium and iron

Papaya helps to calm the digestive system, cucumber flushes out toxins and orange gives a great boost of vitamin C. The overall effect is calming and rehydrating, so all you have to do is take one hot, sticky, over-tired child, add one tumbler of Orange Refresher, then sit back and relax.

Orange refresher

125 g (4 oz) **papaya**
125 g (4 oz) **cucumber**
2 **oranges**

Peel the papaya, cucumber and the oranges (leaving on as much of the pith as possible). Juice them together and serve in a tall glass over ice. Decorate with slices of cucumber and papaya, if liked.

MAKES

Good source of vitamins A and C, magnesium, potassium and selenium

This naturally sweet juice is great if your child has been overdoing it and feels below par. Strawberries are a good source of vitamin C and have antiviral and antibiotic properties, while melon and cucumber both rehydrate and cleanse the system, which is essential for healthy liver, kidneys and adrenal glands.

Cool juice

100 g (3 ½ oz) **strawberries**
75 g (3 oz) **Galia** or **honeydew melon** chunks
75 g (3 oz) **cucumber**

Hull the strawberries, then juice with the melon and cucumber. Serve over ice in a tall glass, decorated with cucumber slices, if liked.

MAKES

Good source of vitamin C, magnesium, potassium, beta-carotene and calcium

If your child is prone to travel sickness, the ginger in this juice will help to alleviate nausea. It also aids digestion and wards off colds – an all-round winner really.

Easy rider

2 **carrots**
1 **apple**, tart-flavoured,
   such as Granny Smith
1 cm (½ in) piece **fresh root ginger**

Cut the carrots, apple and ginger into even-sized pieces and juice. Pour into a glass and add a couple of ice cubes.

MAKES

Good source of vitamins A, C, B$_1$ and B$_6$, potassium, iron and calcium

Juicing is a good way to gradually introduce vegetables into the diets of fussy children, especially when they are combined with sweet fruits. Cucumber is extremely hydrating, making this a great cooling drink for active kids.

Wacky wizard

100 g (3½ oz) **mango**

200 g (7 oz) **apple,** peeled

125 g (4 oz) **cucumber,** peeled

Juice the ingredients and blend with a couple of ice cubes for a fruity slush.

MAKES

Good source of vitamins A and C, calcium and potassium

Technically it is a fruit, but many people classify the nutrient-dense avocado as a vegetable. Whatever its official status, it does make a fantastically complete baby food, especially when combined with gentle pears. If you want to turn this into a tasty smoothie, triple the amount of pear you juice then whiz in a blender with a little ice.

Maybe baby

75 g (3 oz) **avocado**

125 g (4 oz) **pear**

Peel the avocado and remove the stone. Juice the pear and blend with the avocado.

MAKES

Good source of vitamins C, B and E, potassium and magnesium

Perfect for children who love milk but it doesn't love them – a sweet dairy-free treat that will nourish and sustain your child but will not send their blood sugar levels rocketing into orbit.

Wakey-wakey

250 g (8 oz) **pineapple**
100 g (3½ oz) **parsnip**
100 g (3½ oz) **carrot**
75 ml (3 fl oz) **soya milk**

Peel the pineapple, remove the core and cut the flesh into chunks. Juice the pineapple, parsnip and carrot. Whiz in a blender with the soya milk and a couple of ice cubes. Decorate with pineapple wedges, if liked.

MAKES

Good source of vitamin C, potassium, beta-carotene, calcium and folate

Full of iron, calcium and potassium, this non-dairy smoothie is great for bones and teeth and keeping colds at bay. Bananas are also packed with tryptophan which is renowned for its calming properties, so this is a good one to have at the end of a busy day.

Glow in the dark

150 g (5 oz) **carrot**
100 g (3 ½ oz) **orange**
100 g (3 ½ oz) **banana**
6 **dried apricots**

Juice the carrot and orange. Whiz in a blender with the banana, apricots and some ice cubes.

MAKES

Good source of vitamins A and C, calcium, potassium and iron

An ultra-green juice with a sweet flavour and a powerful vitamin punch that will help maintain energy levels and maybe tempt someone who just won't eat their greens.

Green grass

200 g (7 oz) **broccoli**

200 g (7 oz) **apple,** such as Braeburn or Cox

50 g (2 oz) **spinach**

50 g (2 oz) **green grapes**

Roughly chop the broccoli and quarter the apples. Juice everything, then whiz in a blender with a few ice cubes.

MAKES 🥤🥤

Good source of vitamins A and C, selenium and zinc

Super smoothies

Sometimes it's all about the presentation – and this smoothie is well worth the effort. Tasty and bursting with nutrients, it makes a wonderful breakfast treat.

250 g (8 oz) **raspberries**
200 ml (7 fl oz) **apple juice**
200 g (7 oz) **blueberries**
4 tablespoons **Greek yogurt**
100 ml (3½ fl oz) **skimmed milk**
1 tablespoon **clear honey,** or to taste
1 tablespoon **wheatgerm** (optional)

Purée the raspberries with half of the apple juice. Purée the blueberries with the remaining apple juice. Mix together the yogurt, milk, honey and wheatgerm, if using. Add a spoonful of the raspberry purée.

Pour the blueberry purée into the glass. Pour on the yogurt mixture carefully and finally pour the raspberry purée over the surface of the yogurt. Serve chilled.

MAKES

Good source of vitamin C, calcium, iron, magnesium, potassium, phosphorus and zinc

Unless your child is allergic to nuts, this fabulously creamy smoothie will make a fantastic snack that keeps hunger pangs at bay and is so much better than a couple of biscuits or packet of crisps. If your child is lactose intolerant, use rice or soya milk.

Nutty professor

1 **ripe banana**
300 ml (½ pint) **semi-skimmed milk**
1 tablespoon **smooth peanut butter**

Peel and slice the banana, put it in a freezer container and freeze for at least 2 hours or overnight. Put the banana, milk and peanut butter in a blender and whiz until smooth. Serve immediately.

MAKES

Good source of vitamins C, B$_1$, B$_2$, B$_6$ and B$_{12}$, folic acid, niacin, calcium, copper, potassium, zinc, magnesium and phosphorus

This high-carbohydrate, low-fat smoothie is a great choice for refuelling and soothing tired muscles. Bananas are high in potassium, a vital mineral for muscle and nerve function. This is great for breakfast or as a mid-afternoon snack with a flapjack or some oatcakes and hummus.

Starburst

1 **small, ripe banana**
75 g (3 oz) **strawberries**
250 ml (8 fl oz) **orange juice**

Peel the banana and hull the strawberries. Put the fruit into a freezer container and freeze for at least 2 hours or overnight. Place the frozen fruit and the orange juice in a blender and whiz until thick. Decorate with strawberries, if liked, and serve immediately.

MAKES

Great source of vitamins C, B_1 and B_6, folic acid, magnesium, zinc and phosphorus

Summer berries are packed with vitamins C and B. They have a deep colour and rich flavour and so are ideal for making smoothies. Nutritionally, frozen fruit is every bit as good as fresh, and it is available all year round. Soya milk is a good alternative to cows' milk for children who are lactose-intolerant, but look for a calcium-enriched brand for maximum nutrition.

Pink princess

150 g (5 oz) **frozen mixed summer berries**

300 ml (½ pint) **vanilla-flavoured soya milk**

1 teaspoon **clear honey** (optional)

Place the berries, soya milk and honey, if using, in a blender and whiz until thick. Serve immediately, decorated with extra berries, if liked.

MAKES

Great source of vitamins C, B_1, B_2 and B_6, folic acid, copper, potassium, zinc, magnesium, phosphorus, calcium and iron

This smoothie is so thick you might need a spoon to eat it, making it a fantastic summer dessert. Try layering the mango and blackcurrant in an ice-lolly container to make a cooling burst of fruity goodness that children will love.

Purple tiger

3 **mangoes**
2 tablespoons **mango sorbet**
100 ml (3½ fl oz) **apple juice**
200 g (7 oz) **blackcurrants** or **blueberries**

Peel the mangoes, remove the stones and cube the flesh. Purée the mango with the mango sorbet and half the apple juice. Set aside to chill. Purée the blackcurrants with the rest of the apple juice.

To serve, divide the mango smoothie between two glasses. Place a spoon on the surface of the mango, holding it as flat as you can, and pour on the blackcurrant purée. Drag a teaspoon or skewer down the inside of the glass, to make vertical stripes around the glass.

MAKES ⧄⧄

Good source of vitamin C, beta-carotene, potassium, magnesium, zinc and calcium

Juices and smoothies are brilliant for keeping energy levels high when little ones won't eat. Rather than sit a child formally at a dinner table, why not place a glass of this delicious juice within easy reach, along with a few high protein snacks and let them graze for a change – remember battles about food are invariably about pushing boundaries and power struggles.

Tutti-frutti

1 **mango**

3 **apples**, preferably red ones

2 **passionfruits**

Peel the mango and remove the stone. Cut the mango and apples into even-sized pieces. Slice the passionfruits in half, scoop out the flesh and discard the seeds. Juice all the ingredients. Pour the juice into a glass and add a couple of ice cubes, if liked.

MAKES

Good source of vitamins A and C, potassium, magnesium, phosphorus and iron

Traffic light

A colourful thick smoothie that is an excellent source of many nutrients. You can vary the fruits you use – just be sure to stick to the red/amber/green format if you want it to be a true traffic light.

3 **kiwifruits**

150 ml (¼ pint) **tangy flavoured yogurt,** such as lemon or orange

1 **small mango**

2 tablespoons **orange** or **apple juice**

150 g (5 oz) **raspberries**

1–2 teaspoons **clear honey**

Peel and roughly chop the kiwifruits, then whiz in a blender until smooth. Spoon the kiwi mixture into 2 tall glasses. Top each with a spoonful of yogurt, spreading the yogurt to the sides of the glasses.

Peel the mango, remove the stone and roughly chop the flesh. Blend the mango to a purée with the orange or apple juice and spoon into the glasses. Top with another layer of yogurt.

Blend the raspberries and push through a sieve over a bowl to extract the seeds. Check their sweetness. You might need to stir in a little honey if they're very sharp. Spoon the raspberry purée into the glasses.

MAKES

Good source of vitamin C, beta-carotene, potassium, calcium and magnesium

A delicious smoothie that provides calcium to support growing teeth and bones. If your child is lactose intolerant or suffers regularly with colds and sinus problems, use soya yogurt. You can also substitute strawberries or raspberries.

Black beauty

200 g (7 oz) **blackcurrants** or **blackberries**
100 ml (4 fl oz) **apple juice**
300 ml (½ pint) **natural yogurt**
2 tablespoons **clear honey**

If using blackcurrants, remove any stray stalks. Reserve a few pieces of fruit for decoration, then freeze the remainder for 2 hours or overnight.

Whiz the frozen blackcurrants or blackberries in a blender with the apple juice and half the yogurt until combined. Spoon into glasses. Combine the rest of the yogurt with the honey. Spoon over the fruit mixture and serve decorated with the reserved fruit.

MAKES

Good source of vitamin C, calcium and magnesium

This smoothie is an excellent source of calcium, providing almost one-third of the daily requirement. Calcium is essential for helping to build and maintain good bone health, and is also involved in nerve transmission, blood clotting and muscle function. Canned apricots in natural juice are a handy storecupboard standby and provide an extra source of carbohydrate.

Apricot cloud

200 g (7 oz) **can apricots** in natural
juice, drained
150 ml (5 fl oz) **apricot yogurt**
150 ml (¼ pint) **semi-skimmed
milk,** ice-cold

Place the apricots, yogurt and milk in a blender and whiz until smooth. Pour into glasses and decorate with slices of apricot, if liked. Drink immediately.

MAKES

Good source of vitamins A, C, B_1, B_2,
B_6 and $B1_{12}$, calcium,
potassium, zinc,
magnesium and
phosphorus

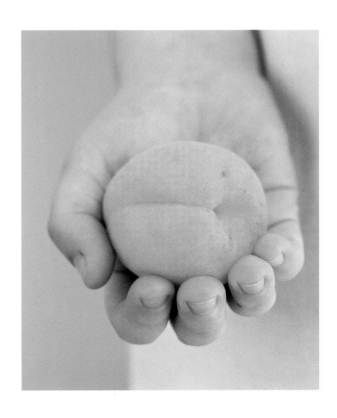

Orange juice is abundant in vitamin C, which is vital for the absorption of iron in the body – a good choice if your child is anaemic or recovering from an illness.

Orange blossom

125 g (4 oz) **strawberries**

1 **small ripe mango**

300 ml (½ pint) **orange juice** or

3 **oranges,** juiced

Hull the strawberries, then freeze for 2 hours or overnight. Peel the mango, remove the stone and roughly chop the flesh. Pour into lolly moulds and freeze until set.

MAKES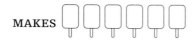

Good source of vitamins A, C, B$_1$, B$_2$ and B$_6$, folic acid, copper, potassium, magnesium and phosphorus, calcium and iron

Bananas are a perfect base for a creamy smoothie and brilliant for active children since they are rich in carbohydrate and potassium. They also contain a special fibre – fructoligosaccharides – that encourages the growth of healthy bacteria in the stomach.

Milky mango

1 **ripe banana**
1 **ripe mango**
200 ml (7 fl oz) **orange juice**
200 ml (7 fl oz) **semi-skimmed milk**
3 tablespoons **fromage frais**

Peel and slice the banana, Peel the mango, remove the stone and roughly chop the flesh. Put the banana, mango, orange juice, milk, fromage frais and a couple of ice cubes in a blender and whiz until smooth. Pour into glasses and serve immediately.

MAKES

Good source of vitamins A, C, B_1, B_2, B_6 and B_{12}, folic acid, calcium, potassium, magnesium and phosphorus

Blackberries and purple grape juice contain antioxidants which are excellent for general health. In addition, purple grape juice is a good source of potassium which is essential for optimum nerve, cell and muscle function. Adding quark or fromage frais gives this drink a creamy taste and texture, and also boosts the calcium and protein content. If you cannot find quark or fromage frais, use natural bio yogurt instead.

Big purple monster

125 g (4 oz) **frozen blackberries**
300 ml (½ pint) **purple grape juice**
3 tablespoons **quark** or **fromage frais**
1 teaspoon **clear honey** (optional)

Put the blackberries, grape juice and quark or fromage frais in a blender, add the honey, if using, and whiz until thick.

MAKES

Good source of vitamins C, B$_1$, B$_2$, B$_6$ and B$_{12}$, folic acid, calcium, iron, magnesium and phosphorus

The combination of bananas, ground almonds and soya milk makes this a highly nutritious drink. It is best to use very ripe bananas (very yellow skin with black spots) as less ripe ones are largely indigestible. Almonds are an excellent source of vitamin E as well as many minerals.

Jumping jack

1 **very ripe banana**
250 ml (8 fl oz) **soya milk**
20 g (¾ oz) **ground almonds**
pinch of **ground cinnamon**
a little **honey** (optional)

Peel and slice the banana, put it into a freezer container and freeze for at least 2 hours or overnight. Place the frozen banana, soya milk, ground almonds and cinnamon in a blender, add the honey, if using, and whiz until thick and frothy. Pour into a glass and serve immediately with ice cubes and decorated with ground cinnamon.

MAKES

Good source of vitamins C, E, B_1, B_2 and B_6, niacin, folic acid, copper, potassium, zinc, magnesium, phosphorus and calcium

No time to prepare fruit? Don't worry – this is a quick, simple-to-make healthy smoothie that can be ready in a minute. Perfect for busy mums and independent kids who want to help in the kitchen, it's high in calcium and immune-boosting beta-carotene.

Easy peachy, orange squeezy

400 g (13 oz) **can peaches** in natural juice, drained

150 ml (¼ pint) **peach** or **apricot yogurt**

200 ml (7 fl oz) **orange juice**

a little **honey** (optional)

Place the peaches in a blender with the yogurt, orange juice and honey, if using, and whiz until smooth. Add a couple of ice cubes, if liked, and top with a swirl of any remaining yoghurt.

MAKES

Good source of vitamins C, B_1, B_2 and B_6, folic acid, calcium, potassium and phosphorus

This is a deliciously sweet, yet refreshing drink and great for rehydration after sports and exercise when energy levels are all used up. If you cannot find passionfruit juice, try using pineapple juice instead.

Little pinky

¼ **watermelon**, about 300 g (10 oz) flesh

2 **kiwifruits**

200 ml (7 fl oz) **passionfruit juice**

Peel and deseed the watermelon and dice the flesh. Put it in a freezer container and freeze for at least 2 hours or overnight.

Peel and roughly chop the kiwifruits then place them in a blender with the watermelon and passionfruit juice and process until thick. Serve immediately.

MAKES

Good source of vitamins A, C, B$_1$, B$_2$ and B$_6$, copper, potassium, zinc, magnesium, phosphorus, iron and calcium

A great, refreshing pick-me-up. Papaya is a good source of vitamin C, beta-carotene, the plant form of vitamin A, and the enzyme papain, which aids digestion in the body. A glass of this will keep your cheeky monkeys full of energy and assist healthy development. A 400 g (13 oz) can of apricot halves in natural juice can be used instead of the papaya and apple juice for a convenient storecupboard version.

Cheeky monkey

1 **papaya**
1 **banana**
1 **orange**
300 ml (½ pint) **apple juice**

Halve and deseed the papaya, then scoop out the flesh with a spoon and put it into a blender. Peel and slice the banana and peel and segment the orange, then place them in the blender with the apple juice and a couple of ice cubes. Whiz until smooth and serve.

MAKES

Good source of vitamins A and C, calcium, potassium, magnesium and iron

A creamy smoothie which is a meal in itself, this is an excellent choice for a recuperating child as avocados are considered a complete food that is easy to digest. When combined with banana and milk, they make a great fuel for growth and repair.

Witches' brew

1 **small ripe avocado**
1 **small ripe banana**
250 ml (8 fl oz) **skimmed milk**

Peel and stone the avocado, and peel the banana. Place the avocado, banana and milk in a blender and whiz until smooth. Pour into a glass, add a couple of ice cubes, decorate with a pineapple wedge, if liked, and serve immediately.

MAKES ▽▽

Good source of vitamins C, E, B_1, B_2, B_6 and B_{12}, folic acid, calcium, potassium, copper, zinc, magnesium and phosphorus

This winning combination can easily be adapted to a storecupboard version using canned peaches or apricots, or you can substitute nectarines for the peaches if they are more readily available. It's a great way to add calcium to the diet of a child who isn't very keen on eating their greens.

Peaches and cream

1 **large peach**
150 ml (¼ pint) **natural yogurt**
50 ml (2 fl oz) **milk**
a few **raspberries**,
to decorate

Peel the peach, remove the stone and roughly chop the flesh. Put the peach, yogurt and milk into a blender and whiz until smooth. Decorate with raspberries.

MAKES

Good source of vitamin C, beta-carotene and zinc

If your child is aching from head to toe and can't seem to function, you need to replace vital potassium and get some vitamin C into their system. They would also probably benefit from some extra B vitamins. This fruity smoothie delivers on all three counts and will help an over-burdened immune system.

Super shaker

100 g (3½ oz) **strawberries**
300 g (10 oz) **pineapple**
1 **banana**

Hull the strawberries. Peel the pineapple, remove the central core and roughly chop the flesh. Juice all the fruit, then pour the juice into a blender, add the banana and a couple of ice cubes and whiz until smooth. Serve decorated with strawberries.

MAKES 🥤🥤

Good source of vitamins C and B, magnesium, potassium and zinc

If your child is over-excited or anxious and can't sleep, a delicious smoothie at bedtime should do the trick. Soya milk and almonds are both very high in tryptophan. This is converted in the body into the brain chemical serotonin, which alleviates insomnia, calms nerves and helps relaxation. This juice is also high in magnesium and vitamin C, making it a good booster for the adrenal glands and immune system.

Sleeping beauty

100 g (3½ oz) **fresh** or **frozen strawberries**

200 ml (7 fl oz) **soya milk**

2 **kiwifruits**

25 g (1 oz) **flaked almonds** (optional)

Hull the strawberries. Put all the ingredients in a blender. If using fresh rather than frozen strawberries add a few ice cubes, then whiz until smooth. Pour into a glass and decorate with flaked almonds, if liked.

MAKES

Good source of vitamins C and E, zinc, tryptophan, calcium and magnesium

This should keep any requests for additive-ridden, sugary thick shakes at bay. It's a bit naughty, but a lot healthier than the burger-bar versions.

Chocolate heaven

1	**banana**
2 tablespoons	**organic cocoa powder**
300 ml (½ pint)	**semi-skimmed milk**
100 ml (3⅓ fl oz)	**apple juice**
2 large scoops	**vanilla ice-cream**

Peel and roughly chop the banana. Put everything in a blender and whiz. Pour into glasses and dust with cocoa powder or chocolate shavings.

MAKES

Good source of vitamin C, calcium, potassium, tryptophan and magnesium

Bananas and mangoes both supply fibre, making this a filling and satisfying smoothie that provides a good source of carbohydrate to fuel activity and refuel afterwards. The yogurt is a very good source of calcium, which is essential for bone health and strength.

Jungle fever

1 **large banana**
1 **large ripe mango**
150 ml (5 fl oz) **natural bio yogurt**
300 ml (½ pint) **pineapple juice**

Peel and slice the banana, then place it in a freezer container and freeze for at least 2 hours or overnight. Peel the mango, remove the stone and cube the flesh. Put the frozen banana, mango, yogurt and pineapple juice into a blender. Whiz until smooth and serve immediately, decorated with a slice of banana, if liked.

MAKES ⎍⎍⎍

Good source of vitamins A, C, B_1, B_2 and B_6, folic acid, calcium, potassium, copper, magnesium and phosphorus

A great all-round smoothie – this is easily absorbed and provides a good energy boost. The bananas and mangoes supply essential fibre and adding yogurt is an effective way to increase the calcium content, which is essential for bone health and strength – truly a bionic tonic.

Bionic tonic

1 **small banana**
½ **large ripe mango**
75 ml (3 fl oz) **natural bio yogurt**
150 ml (¼ pint) **pineapple juice**

Peel and slice the banana, then put it in a freezer container and freeze for at least 2 hours or overnight. Peel the mango, remove the stone and roughly chop the flesh. Place it in a blender with the frozen banana, yogurt and pineapple juice. Whiz until smooth and serve immediately, decorated with pineapple chunks, if liked.

MAKES

Good source of vitamins A, C, B_1, B_2 and B_6, folic acid, potassium, copper, magnesium and phosphorus

Index

Acknowledgements

The publishers would like to thank
Kiara, Michaela, Ellen, Samuel, Charlotte, Daisy, Joshua, Martha, Willoughby, Ellie, Milly, Avni, Charlie, Sam, Ines, Elliot, Frazer, Scarlett, Elsie, Annie, Jack and Imogen for being such wonderful models.

EXECUTIVE EDITOR Nicola Hill
EDITOR Lisa John
CREATIVE DIRECTOR Geoff Fennell
SENIOR PRODUCTION CONTROLLER Ian Paton

SPECIAL PHOTOGRAPHY
© Octopus Publishing Group Limited/ Vanessa Davies
STYLIST Marianne De Vries
HOME ECONOMISTS Cara Hobday and Katie Bishop